What's Happening?

A Book of Explanations

By Patricia Relf
Illustrated by Francis H. Schwartz

For information contact:
MONDO Publishing
980 Avenue of the Americas
New York, New York 10018
Visit our web site at http://www.mondopub.com
Printed in Hong Kong

00 01 02 03 04	HC	9 8 7 6 5 4 3 2 1
00 01 02 03 04	PB	9 8 7 6 5 4 3 2 1
00 01 02 03 04	BB	9 8 7 6 5 4 3 2 1

Design by Vicki Heit
Production by The Kids at Our House

ISBN 1-57255-807-5 (PB)   ISBN 1-57255-841-5 (HC)   ISBN 1-57255-808-3 (BB)

Library of Congress Cataloging-in-Publication data available upon request.

Contents

Introduction

Every day of our lives we turn on water faucets and get clean water. Most days we use a telephone to talk to someone far away. We watch live news from another city on television. We don't give these actions much thought, but there is an amazing story behind each one.

This book explains some of the incredible things that happen in our lives every day. How does a refrigerator make things cold? What makes a car move? We chose ten things that you will probably use or see today. For each one, we show what's happening, step by step.

You will be amazed by the creative inventions that we take for granted every day. Now you will know their hidden stories, and perhaps you will look at other marvelous things around you with a new curiosity.

Have fun finding out what's happening!

Glass

1. Beach sand is mostly tiny bits of *silica*. Glass is made from the silica in sand. First, the sand is cleaned and ground into even tinier bits.

CLEANED   **GROUND**

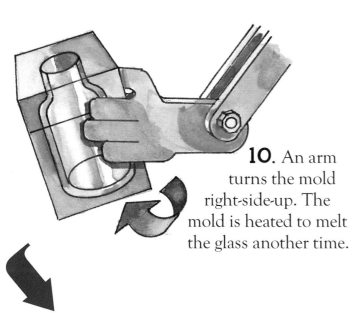

10. An arm turns the mold right-side-up. The mold is heated to melt the glass another time.

9. A machine blows a strong puff of air into the mold to make the space bigger.

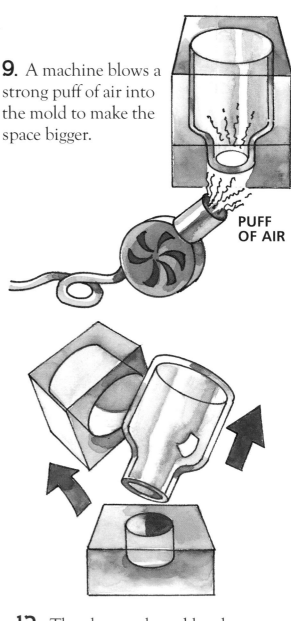

PUFF OF AIR

11. Again, a machine blows air into the mold to make the walls of the jar thin and even.

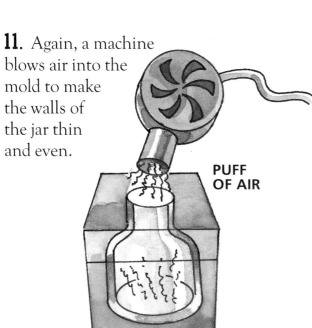

PUFF OF AIR

12. The glass cools and hardens. The jar is removed from the mold.

2. Glassmakers add a gray powder containing *soda ash* and *lime*, which is like chalk. This powder will help the sand to melt more easily.

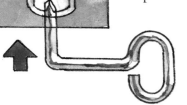

SODA ASH AND LIME

3. In a big bin, a mixing machine stirs the sand, soda ash, and lime together.

STIRRED

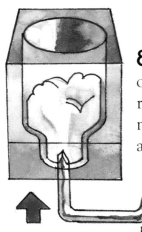

8. From the bottom of the mold, a metal rod pokes the glob of melted glass to make a space in the center.

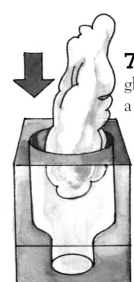

7. The melted glass drops into a *mold*.

The mold is shaped like an upside-down jar.

13. The jar is heated again, then cooled very slowly. This keeps the glass from cracking later.

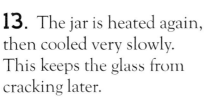

HEATED AGAIN

14. Glass makes a good container. It can be cleaned easily and it lets people see what is inside.

4. The mixture goes to a tank where it is heated to a very high temperature. The tank is five times as hot as an oven at home.

HEATED

5. The powders melt to make very hot liquid glass. Even when it is liquid, melted glass is thick. It does not pour like water.

6. To make a glass jar, a machine with metal blades, like big scissors, cuts off a glob of liquid glass.

15. You can *recycle* glass jars and bottles. Clean, broken bits of glass can be melted and molded all over again.

3. The water flows through layers of sand and gravel to take out any dirt that is left.

4. A little *chlorine* is added to kill microscopic plants and animals, and any harmful germs.

PINCH OF CHLORINE ADDED

5. The water is pumped to a water tower. This huge tank of water is up high. *Gravity* pulls the water through pipes to your house.

6. A big underground pipe, called a *water main*, brings the clean water to your neighborhood. Smaller pipes carry water into your house.

MICROSCOPIC ANIMAL EATING BAD GERM

15. The clean water is then pumped out into a river, lake, or ocean.

Refrigerator

1. A refrigerator is an invention that removes heat from inside a box and sends it to the outside air. Food inside a refrigerator stays cold.

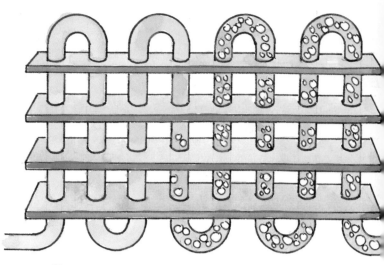

2. A liquid called a *coolant* runs through tubes inside the refrigerator. This coolant is a special chemical that boils even when it is very cold.

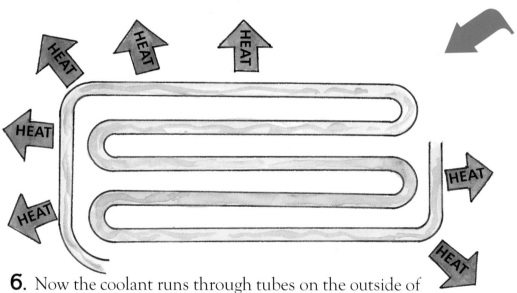

6. Now the coolant runs through tubes on the outside of the refrigerator so that the heat goes to the outside air. You can see these tubes and feel the heat coming from them.

EVAPORATOR

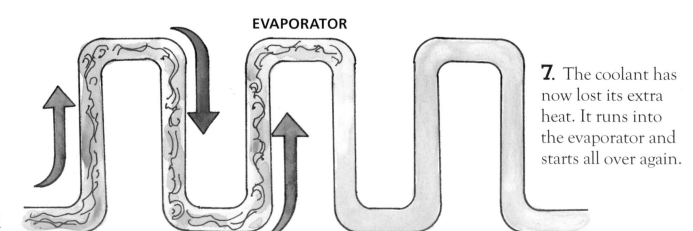

7. The coolant has now lost its extra heat. It runs into the evaporator and starts all over again.

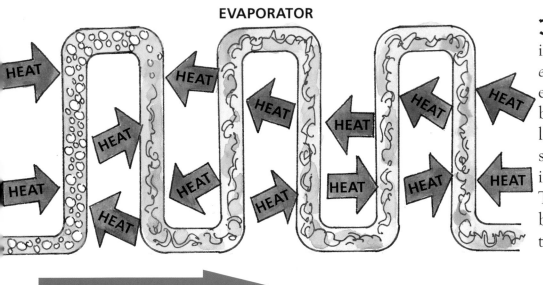

EVAPORATOR

3. Inside the refrigerator is a machine called an *evaporator*. Inside the evaporator, the coolant boils and turns to a gas, like water turning to steam. Liquids need heat in order to turn to gas. The coolant turns to gas by taking heat from inside the refrigerator.

5. The coolant, which is a gas now, runs into a machine called a *compressor*. The compressor presses on the coolant so that it turns back into a liquid. When a gas turns back to a liquid, it gives off heat.

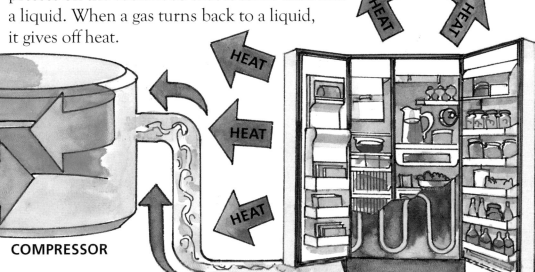

COMPRESSOR

4. When the coolant takes heat away, the inside of the refrigerator becomes cold. Heat is taken away from the air inside, and from all the food in the freezer and refrigerator.

8. When the air inside the refrigerator starts to get warm, the *thermostat* switches on the refrigerator. When the air inside is cold enough, it switches off the refrigerator.

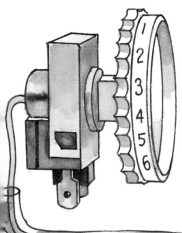

9. The walls of the refrigerator are thick. Rubber seals keep the door closed tightly. This helps to keep heat out and cold air inside the refrigerator.

13

Telephone

1. When you talk, you send sound waves from your throat into the air.

2. When you talk into a telephone, the sound waves hit a thin metal plate and make it shake, or *vibrate*.

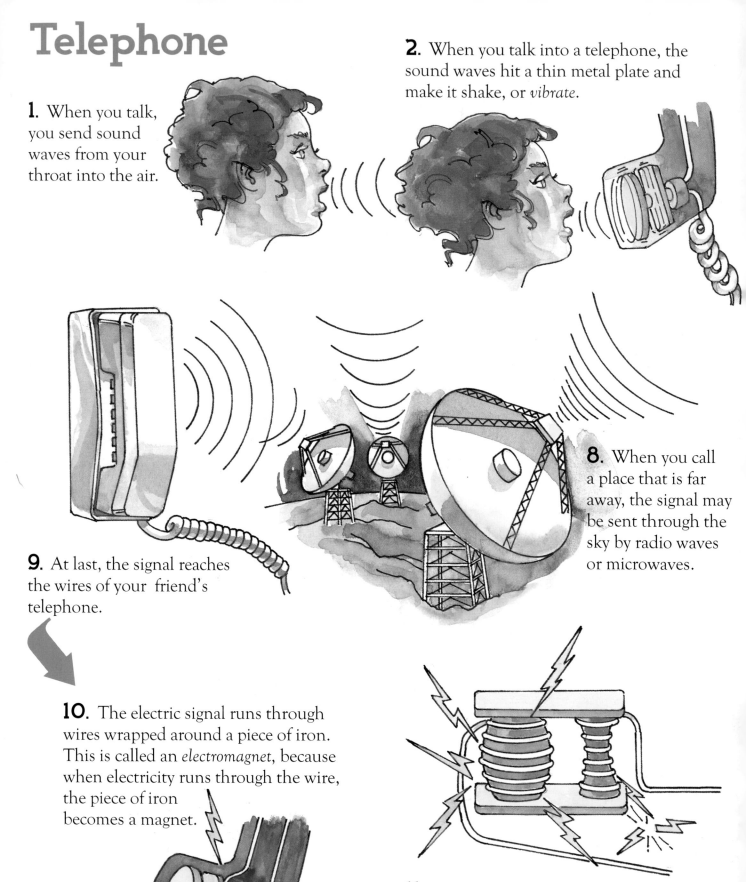

8. When you call a place that is far away, the signal may be sent through the sky by radio waves or microwaves.

9. At last, the signal reaches the wires of your friend's telephone.

10. The electric signal runs through wires wrapped around a piece of iron. This is called an *electromagnet*, because when electricity runs through the wire, the piece of iron becomes a magnet.

11. Remember, the electricity that came from your telephone is sometimes weak and sometimes strong. So the magnet is sometimes weak and sometimes strong, too.

CARBON GRANULES

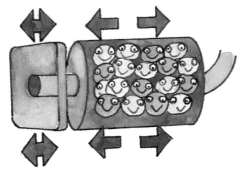

4. When your voice shakes the metal plate, sometimes the plate presses hard on the bits of carbon. They squash together, and more electricity flows through the carbon.

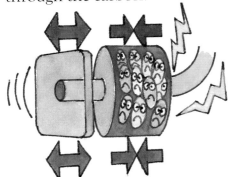

3. Behind the metal plate, there are small bits of *carbon*. They look a little like tiny pieces of charcoal. Electricity runs from a wire, through the carbon, and out through another wire.

5. Sometimes as the metal plate vibrates, it presses more lightly. The bits of carbon are loose. Then less electricity flows through the carbon.

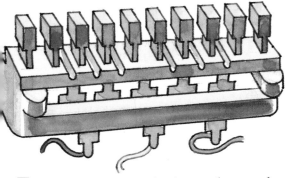

7. The signal travels through metal or special glass wires. Switches send the signal to different wires so that it will reach the person you are calling.

6. So, sometimes the electricity is strong, and sometimes it is weak. The strong and weak electricity is a *signal*, like a code of your voice. The strong and weak electricity travels through a wire to the telephone.

13. The magnet makes the metal plate shake or vibrate. The shaking metal plate sends sound waves to your friend's ear. It shakes just the way the plate in your telephone shook when you talked. It sounds just like you!

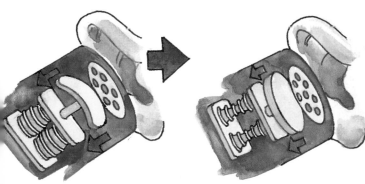

12. This telephone has another thin metal plate, right next to your friend's ear. When the magnet is strong, it pulls hard on that metal plate. When the magnet is weak, it only pulls lightly.

Television

1. At the television studio, light bounces off the actors and objects. The light enters the television camera through the camera's lens.

2. The lens points the light onto a *signal plate* inside the camera. This plate has thousands of tiny spots in many rows. The light that hits each spot changes it. The spot senses how bright the light is and whether the light contains any blue, red, or green color. Different combinations of these three colors of light can make any color.

BLUE, RED, GREEN BEAMS

6. The signal goes to three *electron guns* inside the back of your television. Each gun creates a different color—blue, red, and green. The guns shoot out beams of electrons that move across the television screen 30 times a second.

7. The television screen is made of thousands of tiny colored strips. When the electron beam from the blue gun hits a blue strip, the screen glows blue in that spot. When the electron beams from all three guns hit a spot on the screen, the colors mix, and that spot looks white. If you look closely at a television picture, you can see the rows of tiny colored dots.

3. A beam of tiny particles called *electrons* zips across the rows of spots 30 times a second. That's fast!

4. Every time the beam of electrons passes a spot, it sends out a signal about how bright that spot is and what colors it contains.

5. The signal travels to your television. It can go straight to your TV antenna. Or, it may travel up to a *satellite*, then back down to your satellite dish. Or, the signal can travel underground through a cable.

8. When you sit a few feet away from the television, the tiny dots blend together to make a picture.

17

Mail

1. You write a letter to a friend. You put it in an envelope, write your friend's address on the front, and stick on a stamp. The stamp shows that you have paid for your letter's trip.

2. You drop the letter in a mailbox.

9. The bags and boxes of mail are loaded onto trucks. Mail for faraway places goes to the airport. The bags of mail are loaded onto airplanes to fly to different places.

8. Now a machine called a *bar code sorter* can separate the envelopes into different bags or boxes. Mail in each bag or box is going to a different place.

| CITY | STATE | COUNTRY |

10. There, the bags are unloaded from the truck or airplane and loaded onto another truck. They go to the sorting office.

TO SORTING OFFICE

My Friend
Street Address
Anytown, U.S.A.
　　　　60609

FOR POST OFFICE NEAR YOUR FRIEND'S HOME

11. The bar code sorter reads the code of black lines on your letter. The sorter drops your letter into a bag with other letters for the post office near your friend's home.

E-mail

1. The *Internet* makes it possible for a computer to "talk" to another computer that may be far away. *E-mail* means "electronic mail."

6. The signal for your message travels through telephone lines, which can be copper wires or special glass cables. If it has a long way to go, the signal may be changed to a radio signal so that it can travel through the sky. It may even bounce off a satellite in space.

7. Your message reaches the hub that is closest to your friend's computer. The huge computer at this hub reads the address. It sends the message to your friend's Internet service provider.

4. The message goes first to a big computer at the office of your *Internet service provider.*

5. The big computer sends the message to a *hub*, which is a huge computer that sorts out messages from many different providers. This computer reads the address on your message. It sends the message to another hub.

8. The computer at your friend's provider sends the message to your friend's computer.

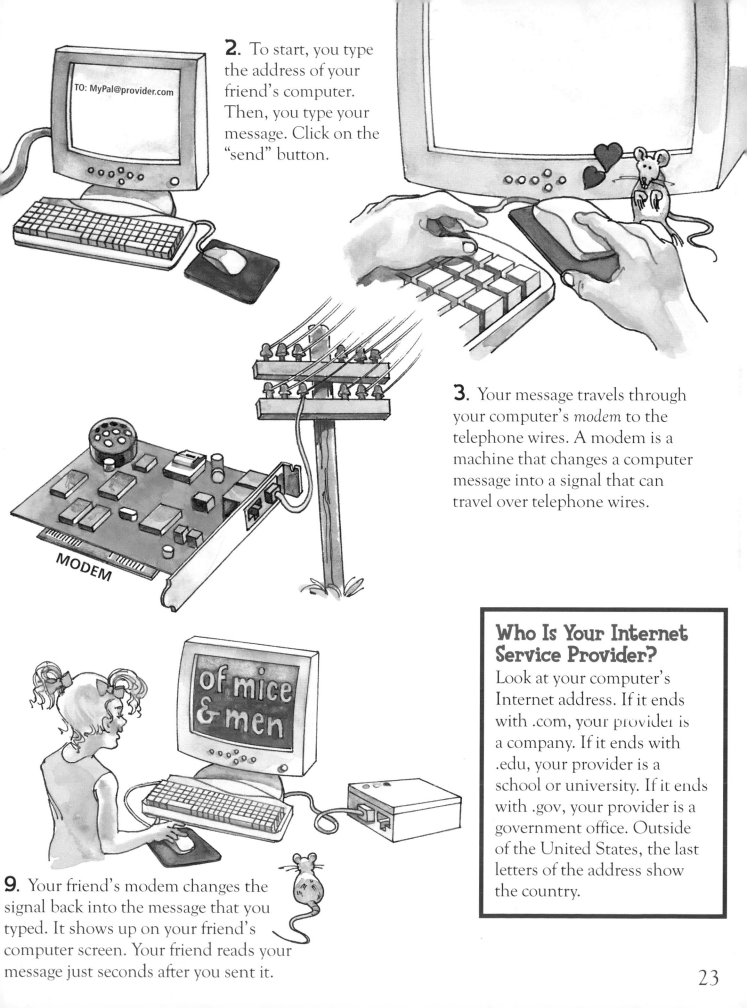

2. To start, you type the address of your friend's computer. Then, you type your message. Click on the "send" button.

TO: MyPal@provider.com

3. Your message travels through your computer's *modem* to the telephone wires. A modem is a machine that changes a computer message into a signal that can travel over telephone wires.

MODEM

Who Is Your Internet Service Provider?

Look at your computer's Internet address. If it ends with .com, your provider is a company. If it ends with .edu, your provider is a school or university. If it ends with .gov, your provider is a government office. Outside of the United States, the last letters of the address show the country.

9. Your friend's modem changes the signal back into the message that you typed. It shows up on your friend's computer screen. Your friend reads your message just seconds after you sent it.

of mice & men

Newspaper Recycling

1. Paper is made from trees. People can save trees by recycling paper. Here's how it works. You read today's newspaper.

2. Instead of throwing the paper in the trash, you put it with other old newspapers.

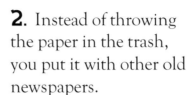

NEWSPAPERS ONLY!

9. The processor packs and ties up the old papers into huge bales.

8. The processor sorts the papers, taking out dirty paper, pieces of metal or glass, and anything else that cannot be made into new paper.

10. At a mill, the papers go into a vat. Water and chemicals are added to remove the ink. Some new material from trees may be added, too.

WATER   CHEMICALS

11. A machine sprays the watery, mushy *slurry* between two fabric rollers. As the rollers turn, they squeeze water out. Then steel rollers press the paper to make it flat, dry, and smooth.

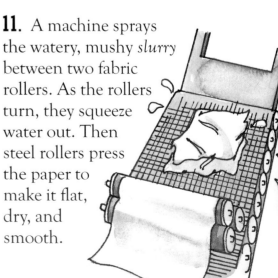

3. On recycling day, you put the pile of papers outside.

4. A recycling truck stops at your house. The driver loads your old newspapers into a special bin in the truck.

Newspapers Plastics

SANITATION

5. The driver takes all the newspapers to a transfer station.

7. The truck delivers the old newspapers to a processor.

SANITATION

6. The driver moves all the newspapers into a big truck.

13. The paper runs through the printing press. Out comes a new newspaper. Recycling old newspapers saves trees!

12. A machine winds the new paper onto cardboard tubes. Trucks take the big rolls of new paper to a printing plant.

Car Engine

2. As the car drives away, a *fuel pump* sends gasoline from the car's tank to the engine.

GAS TANK

1. Most cars use *gasoline* for energy. Gasoline stored in an underground tank at the gas station goes through a pump into your car's gas tank.

SPARK PLUG

PISTON

6. The explosion pushes hard against the piston. The piston moves down. It pushes on an arm called the crankshaft. It makes the crankshaft turn.

7. The crankshaft turns gears in the car's *transmission*. The gears turn the car's *axles*. So the piston's hard push turns the wheels of the car, which makes it go.

CRANKSHAFT

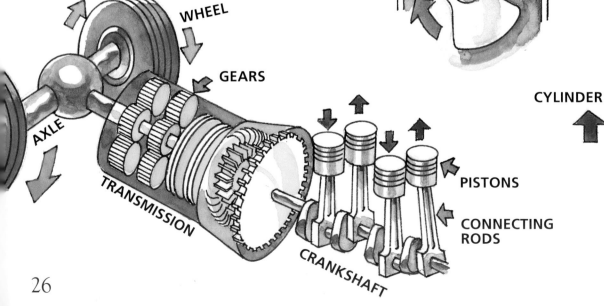

WHEEL

GEARS

AXLE

TRANSMISSION

CRANKSHAFT

PISTONS

CONNECTING RODS

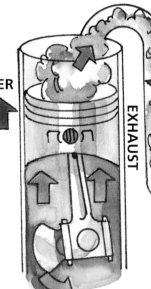

CYLINDER

EXHAUST

3. A *fuel injector* sprays the gasoline into a *cylinder*. This spray mixes with air. It can explode very easily.

4. Inside the cylinder, a *piston* moves up and down. The piston pushes on the spray of gasoline. Now the spray can explode even more easily.

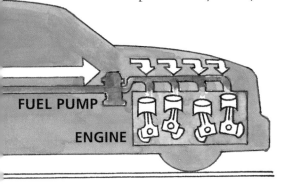

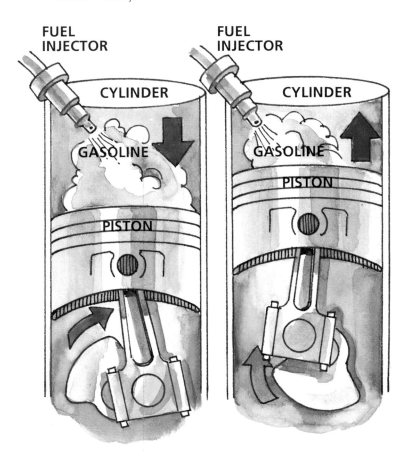

5. At just the right moment, a spark plug makes an electrical spark. The gasoline spray explodes!

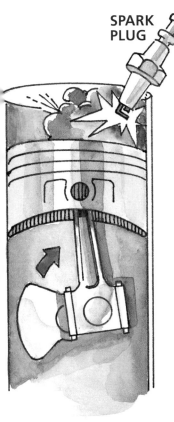

9. Your car has four, six, or eight cylinders. The pistons in these cylinders take turns pushing. Explosions in the cylinders happen many times each minute.

8. When the piston pushes into the cylinder again, it pushes out the smoke from the explosion. The exhaust goes through a muffler to make the car quieter, then it goes out through a pipe at the back of the car.

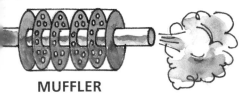

MUFFLER

27

Jet Engine

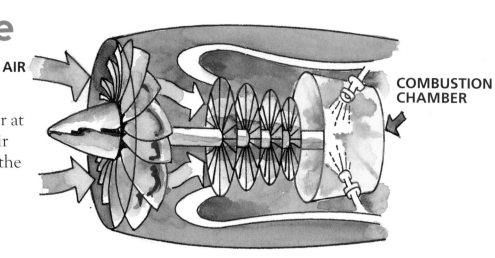

AIR

COMBUSTION CHAMBER

1. A jet engine sucks in air at its front. Fans press the air together and send it into the *combustion* chamber.

5. Like air shooting out of a balloon, the gases shoot out the back of the engine and push the airplane forward.

6. As the airplane moves forward, air flows over and under the wings.

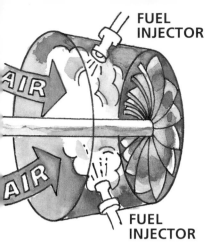

FUEL INJECTOR

FUEL INJECTOR

2. There, the air mixes with jet *fuel*. Jet fuel is like the kerosene that some lamps and heaters burn.

3. The fuel burns and sends a strong jet of gases out the back of the engine.

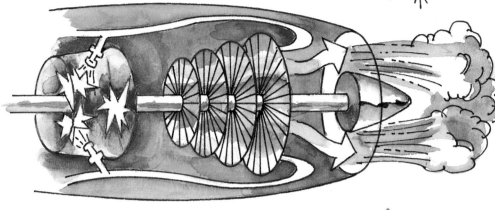

FRONT OF JET ENGINE

TURBINE

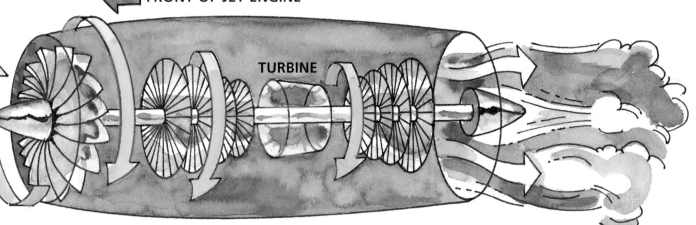

4. As the gases shoot out, they turn a *turbine*, which turns the fans at the front of the engine.

7. An airplane wing has a special shape. The air that flows under the wing moves in a straight line. The air that flows over the wing must travel over a curve. It travels farther, so it must travel faster. Air that is traveling faster presses more lightly.

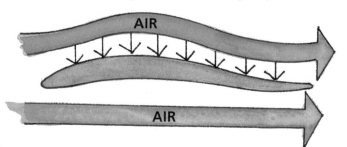

AIR

AIR

AIR

AIR

AIR

8. The air under the wing presses harder than the air on top of the wing. So, as the airplane moves forward, the air under the wing lifts the airplane up . . . up . . . up!

29

Glossary

access cover: a flat lid in a road or sidewalk, also called a manhole cover. It opens to let workers reach underground pipes and cables.

axle: a rod on which wheels rotate.

bar code: a coded pattern of black lines that are printed on an envelope so that a machine can tell where a letter is going.

bar code sorter: a machine that reads the bar code on a letter and sorts the letter according to where it is going.

carbon: an element found in all living things. Coal, charcoal, and diamonds are made mostly or entirely of carbon.

combustion: the burning of fuel.

compressor: a machine that presses gas together to turn it into a liquid.

coolant: a liquid or gas that absorbs heat and carries the heat away.

cylinder: a long, round shape like a jar or a barrel that is sometimes hollow inside.

electricity: a motion of charged particles, such as electrons; a form of energy or power. Electricity passes through wires to carry energy from one place to another.

electrons: tiny particles, usually parts of an atom.

evaporator: a machine that turns liquid to gas. This process requires heat.

fuel: something that burns to give energy.

gasoline: a liquid that catches fire or explodes easily, that is used as fuel for cars, lawn mowers, etc. It comes from oil, or petroleum, found underground.

gravity: the force that tends to pull things down, toward the center of the earth. Without gravity, we would float off the earth.

Internet: an organized way for computer users and networks around the world to communicate with each other.

Internet service provider: a company that connects your computer with the other computers on the Internet; also called an ISP.

microscopic: so small that you would need a microscope to see it. Most germs are microscopic.

optical character reader: a machine that detects the shapes of letters, used to read addresses and other printed words; also called an OCR.

piston: a solid piece of metal that fits tightly inside a cylinder. When it pushes into the cylinder, it moves or compresses the gas or liquid inside.

satellite: a machine sent into space to circle around the earth. It receives signals from earth and sends them back to another place on earth.

signal: a communication; in telephones, radios, and televisions, a sound wave, radio wave, or electrical pulse sent through the air or a wire.

silica: a material found in quartz rocks and sand. In powder form, it is used to make glass, ceramics, and sandpaper.

slurry: small bits of solids mixed into a liquid to make them pourable or spreadable.

thermostat: a special switch that keeps something at a particular temperature.

transmission: in a car or truck, a set of gears that sends turning power from the crankshaft to the wheels with the right strength and speed.

turbine: a wheel of blades that turns when a stream of gas or liquid rushes past.

Index